crocheted Scraps to Beauty Afghans

Those of us who do a great deal of crocheting, constantly find ourselves with leftover odds and ends of yarn. In this leaflet we have offered you 3 designs that encourage you to use up all of those scraps while creating something beautiful and useful an afghan. In addition, we wanted you to see the versatility of these crochet patterns, so we have shown the same 3 designs worked in planned color schemes. You will see that by varying the color combinations, you can create entirely different looks. Beginning crocheters will find the instructions for these afghans exceptionally easy to follow. They are written using no abbreviations and we have taken special care to explain every step as fully as possible, using diagrams whenever we felt this would add to the clarity.

TABLE OF CONTENT

LEISURE ARTS, INC. • Maumelle, Arkansas

MULTI-COLOR TIER DROP

MULTI-COLOR TIER DROP

designed by Ginna Brizendine; Knit 'n Stitch, Little Rock, AR

SIZE: Approximately 48" x 65" before fringing

VERSION A *(Shown on page 2)*

MATERIALS

Worsted weight yarn, 14 ounces (397.6 grams) light rust, 12 ounces (340.8 grams) each brown, ecru and dark rust; aluminum crochet hook size J (Canadian size 3) **or** size needed for gauge.

GAUGE: In double crochet, 3 stitches = 1"; 2 rows = 1"

Stripe Pattern

2 rows light rust

2 rows dark rust

2 rows brown

2 rows ecru

INSTRUCTIONS

Note: Chain 3 **(turning chain)** counts as first double crochet.

With light rust chain 145 loosely.

Row 1: Double crochet in fourth chain from hook and in next chain, ★ chain 1, skip next chain, double crochet in each of next 3 chains; repeat from ★ across; chain 3, turn **(now and throughout)**.

Row 2: Double crochet in each of next 2 double crochets, ★ chain 1, double crochet in each of next 3 double crochets; repeat from ★ across, ending by working double crochet in top of turning chain until 2 loops remain on hook, **change colors as follows**: cut light rust leaving 4" strand to be woven in later, pick up dark rust and draw thru remaining 2 loops **(color change made)**.

Row 3: ★ Chain 1, skip next double crochet, double crochet in next double crochet, **work Long double crochet as follows**: yarn over, insert hook in next chain-1 space 2 rows below ***(Figure 1)***, pull up a ¾" loop, (yarn over and draw thru 2 loops) twice **(Long double crochet made)**, double crochet in next double crochet; repeat from ★ across to last double crochet, chain 1, skip next double crochet, double crochet in top of turning chain.

Figure 1

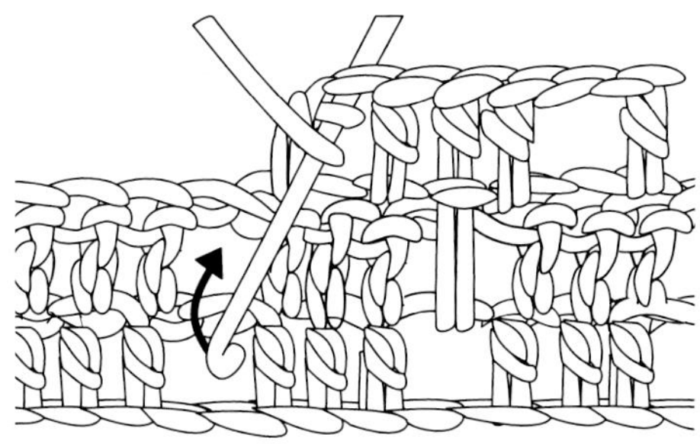

Row 4: ★ Chain 1, double crochet in each of next 3 double crochets; repeat from ★ across, ending chain 1, double crochet in top of turning chain, changing colors as before to brown.

Row 5: Work Long double crochet, double crochet in next double crochet, ★ chain 1, skip next double crochet, double crochet in next double crochet, work Long double crochet, double crochet in next double crochet; repeat from ★ across, ending double crochet in top of turning chain.

Row 6: Double crochet in each of next 2 double crochets, ★ chain 1, double crochet in each of next 3 double crochets; repeat from ★ across, ending double crochet in top of turning chain, changing colors as before to ecru.

Repeat Rows 3-6, following color sequence in Stripe Pattern and changing colors as instructed until piece measures approximately 65", ending by working 2 rows light rust.

Finishing

FRINGE

Following Basic Fringe Instructions, page 12, cut 16" strands of light rust. Use 6 strands for each knot and tie 1 knot in each chain-1 space across each short end.

VERSION B *(Shown on page 2)*

MATERIALS

Worsted weight yarn, 50 ounces (1420 grams) assorted colors; aluminum crochet hook size J {Canadian size 3) **or** size needed for gauge.

Materials Note: 2 rows in pattern require approximately 35 yards of one color.

GAUGE: In double crochet, 3 stitches = 1"; 2 rows = 1"

INSTRUCTIONS

Working 2 rows in each color, work same as VERSION A.

Fringe with beginning and ending colors.

Alternate Color Schemes

Alternate #1

Yarn Requirements: Worsted weight yarn, 26 ounces (738.4 grams) dark grey, 12 ounces (340.8 grams) **each** light grey and white.

Working Instructions: Beginning and ending with 2 rows dark grey, work Stripe Pattern of 2 rows dark grey, 2 rows white, 2 rows dark grey, 2 rows light grey.

Fringe with dark grey.

Alternate #2

Yarn Requirements: Worsted weight yarn, 32 ounces (908.8 grams) medium grey, 16 ounces (454.4 grams) dark red.

Working Instructions: Beginning and ending with 2 rows dark red, work Stripe Pattern of 2 rows dark red, 6 rows medium grey.

Fringe with dark red.

RIBBONS OF COLOR

designed by John Fedderson, Jr.;
The Spinning Wheel, Tuscon, AZ

SIZE: Approximately 47" x 65" before finishing

VERSION A *(Shown on page 6)*

MATERIALS

Worsted weight yarn, 28 ounces (795.2 grams) light beige, 8 ounces (227.2 grams) **each** medium brown and dark brown, 4 ounces (113.6 grams) **each** cream, rust, medium yellow and dark gold; aluminum crochet hook size J (Canadian size 3) **or** size needed for gauge.

GAUGE: In double crochet, 3 stitches = 1"; 2 rows = 1"
In (double crochet, chain 1) mesh,
3 stitches = 1"; 2 rows = 1"

INSTRUCTIONS

Note: Chain 3 **(turning chain)** counts as first double crochet.

With light beige chain 197 loosely.

Row 1: Double crochet in fourth chain from hook and in each chain across; chain 3, turn: 195 double crochets.

Row 2: Double crochet in second double crochet and in each double crochet across, working last double crochet in top of turning chain; chain 3, turn: 195 double crochets.

Rows 3 and 4: Repeat Row 2 twice; at end of Row 4, chain 4, turn **(counts as double crochet plus 1 chain)**.

Note: Take care to maintain proper gauge while working mesh rows.

Row 5: ★ Skip second double crochet, double crochet in next double crochet, chain 1; repeat from ★ across, ending double crochet in top of turning chain; chain 4, turn.

Row 6: ★ Skip next chain-1 space, double crochet in next double crochet, chain 1; repeat from ★ across, ending skip first chain of turning chain, double crochet in next chain; chain 4, turn.

Rows 7-10: Repeat Row 6, 4 times; at end of Row 10, chain 3, turn.

Row 11: Double crochet in each chain-1 space and in each double crochet across, ending double crochet in last space, skip first chain, double crochet in next chain of turning chain; chain 3, turn.

Rows 12-14: Repeat Row 2, 3 times; at end of Row 14, chain 4, turn.

Repeat Rows 5-14, 8 times. At end of last row, do not chain; finish off. Weave in yarn ends.

Finishing

WEAVING

For 1 woven stripe, cut 2 strands **each** medium brown and dark brown and 1 strand **each** cream, rust, medium yellow and dark gold the length of your afghan, allowing several inches to be taken up by weaving plus 18" to be used as fringe.

Row 1: With piece **right** side facing and 1 long side at top, weave all 8 strands together from **right** to **left** thru first row of mesh, beginning over first double crochet, ★ under next double crochet, over next double crochet; repeat from ★ across, leaving approximately 9" at **each** end.

Row 2: Beginning again at right edge of afghan, weave all 8 strands together, under first double crochet, ★ over next double crochet, under next double crochet; repeat from ★ across as before.

Continue in same manner, using same number of strands to weave thru each mesh row on afghan.

FRINGE

Using overhand knot ***(Figure 2)***, tie loose ends of woven strands from first and second mesh rows together to form a knot of fringe.

In same manner, tie loose strands from each 2 woven rows across both short ends of afghan.

Cut 18" strands in same amount and colors as used for each woven row. Evenly spacing 2 knots in each end of double crochet rows between each mesh section, pull 1 end of all strands for 1 knot together thru last stitch in end of double crochet row; fold in half and tie same as woven strands.

Trim ends evenly.

Figure 2

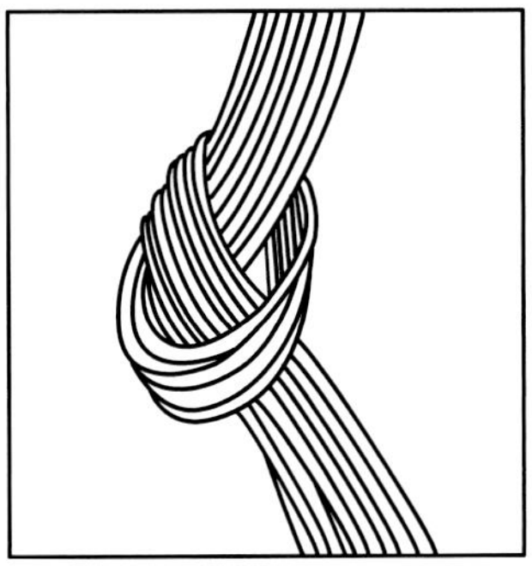

RIBBONS OF COLOR

VERSION B *(Shown on page 6)*

MATERIALS

Worsted weight yarn, 54 ounces (1533.6 grams) assorted colors; aluminum crochet hook size J (Canadian size 3) **or** size needed for gauge.

Materials Note: 2 rows in double crochet require approximately 45 yards; 6 row: in mesh require approximately 90 yards.

GAUGE: In double crochet, 3 stitches = 1"; 2 rows = 1"
In (double crochet, chain 1) mesh,
3 stitches = 1" ; 2 rows = 1"

INSTRUCTIONS

Note: Use medium and dark colors for crochet; use lighter colors for woven strands.

Rows 1 and 2: With desired color, chain and work Rows 1 and 2 same as VERSION A, page 5. At end of Row 2, **change color as follows**: work last double crochet until 2 loops remain on hook, drop old color, with new color complete double crochet; chain 3, turn.

Rows 3 and 4: With new color, work same as VERSION A Rows 3 and 4. At end of last row, join new color as before, chain 4, turn.

Rows 5-10: With new color, work same as VERSION A Rows 5-10; at end of Row 10, change color as before; chain 3, turn.

Continuing to work each 2 double crochet rows in 1 color and all 6 mesh rows in 1 color, complete same as VERSION A.

Finishing

Using light colors for woven strands, cut strands; weave and fringe same as VERSION A.

Alternate Color Schemes

Alternate #1

Yarn Requirements: Worsted weight yarn,
28 ounces (795.2 grams) ombre yarn and
32 ounces (908 grams) white.

Working Instructions: Work all crochet in ombre.

Weave strands of white thru mesh rows.

Fringe with white.

Alternate #2

Yarn Requirements: Worsted weight yarn,
24 ounces (681.6 grams) light green,
14 ounces (397.6 grams) pale green,
8 ounces (227.2 grams) each medium and dark green.

Working Instructions: Work double crochet rows in light green and mesh rows in pale green.

Use 2 strands light green and 3 strands **each** medium and dark green for woven strands.

Fringe with 2 strands light green and 3 strands **each** medium and light green.

KALEIDOSCOPE

KALEIDOSCOPE

designed by Mary B. Caldwell; Rome, GA

SIZE: Approximately 45" x 65" without tassels or fringe

VERSION A (*Shown on page 8*)

MATERIALS

Worsted weight yarn, 30 ounces (852 grams) medium yellow, 18 ounces (511.2 grams) orange, 11 ounces (312.4 grams) dark rust; aluminum crochet hook size H (Canadian size 5) **or** size needed for gauge.

GAUGE: In double crochet, 4 stitches = 1"; 2 rows = 1"
Rounds 1-6 = 6¼" x 8" hexagon

Pattern Stitch

Front Post Double Triple Crochet: Yarn over 3 times, insert hook from **front** to **back** and out to **front** again around post of double crochet 2 rows **below** ***(Figure 3)***, hook yarn and pull up a loop (5 loops on hook), (yarn over and draw thru 2 loops) 4 times, skip double crochet **behind** Front Post double triple crochet **(Front Post double triple crochet completed)**.

Figure 3

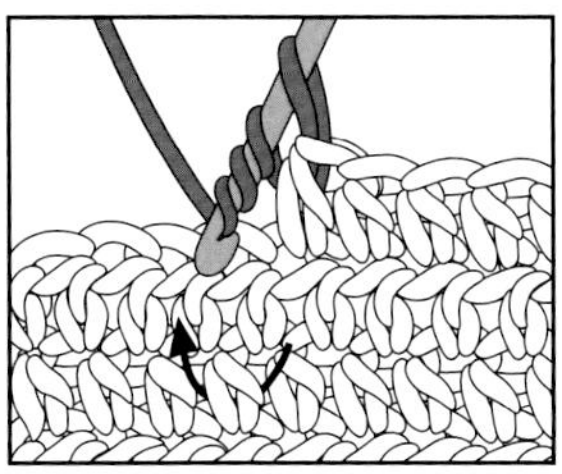

INSTRUCTIONS

Hexagon Motif (Make 72)

With dark rust chain 6; join with slip stitch in beginning chain to form a ring.

Round 1: Chain 3 **(counts as first double crochet)**, 2 double crochets in ring, chain 1, (3 double crochets in ring, chain 1) 5 times; join with slip stitch in third chain of beginning chain-3 **(now and throughout unless otherwise specified)**: 6, 3-double crochet groups.

Round 2: Work beginning increase as follows: chain 3, double crochet in same stitch as joining **(beginning increase made)**, double crochet in next double crochet, **increase as follows**: 2 double crochets in next double crochet **(increase made)**, chain 1, skip next chain-1 space, (increase in next double crochet, double crochet in next double crochet, increase in next double crochet, chain 1, skip next chain-1 space) 5 times; finish off.

Round 3: Join orange with slip stitch in first double crochet to left of any chain-1 space; work beginning increase, double crochet in next double crochet, work Front Post double triple crochet around post of center double crochet in 3-double crochet group 2 rows **below**, double crochet in next double crochet, increase in next double crochet, chain 1, skip next chain-1 space, (increase in next double crochet, double crochet in next double crochet, work Front Post double triple crochet as before, double crochet in next double crochet, increase in next double crochet, chain 1, skip next chain-1 space) 5 times.

Round 4: Work beginning increase, double crochet in next 5 stitches **(working in top of Front Post double triple crochet same as in each double crochet)**, increase in next double crochet, chain 1, skip next chain-1 space, (increase in next double crochet, double crochet in next 5 stitches, increase in next double crochet, chain 1, skip next chain-1 space) 5 times; finish off.

Round 5: Join yellow same as orange; work beginning increase, double crochet in next double crochet, work Front Post double triple crochet around post of second double crochet of increase 2 rows **below**, double crochet in next 3 double crochets, work Front Post double triple crochet around post of first double crochet of next increase 2 rows **below**, double crochet in next double crochet, increase in next double crochet, chain 1, skip next chain-1 space, (increase in next double crochet, double crochet in next double crochet, work Front Post double triple crochet as before, double crochet in next 3 double crochets, work Front Post double triple crochet, double crochet in next double crochet, increase in next double crochet, chain 1, skip next chain-1 space) 5 times.

Round 6: Work beginning increase, double crochet in next 9 stitches, increase in next double crochet, chain 1, skip next chain-1 space, (increase in next double crochet, double crochet in next 9 stitches, increase in next double crochet, chain 1, skip next chain-1 space) 5 times; finish off.

Weave in yarn ends.

Half Motif (Make 10)

Note: All rows are worked on **right** side with yarn finished off at end of each row.

Row 1: With dark rust chain 4, (2 double crochets, chain 1, 3 double crochets, chain 1, 3 double crochets) in fourth chain from hook; finish off.

Row 2: Join dark rust with slip stitch in last chain of chain-4 on previous row; **work beginning increase as follows**: chain 3, double crochet in same chain as joining **(beginning increase made)**, double crochet in next double crochet, **increase as follows**: 2 double crochets in next double crochet **(increase made)**, chain 1, skip next chain-1 space, increase in next double crochet, double crochet in next double crochet, increase in next double crochet, chain 1, skip next chain-1 space, increase in next double crochet, double crochet in next double crochet, increase in remaining double crochet; finish off.

Row 3: Join orange with slip stitch in third chain of beginning chain-3 on previous row; work beginning increase, (double crochet in next double crochet, work Front Post double triple crochet around post of center double crochet in 3-double crochet group 2 rows **below**, double crochet in next double crochet, increase in next double crochet, chain 1, skip next chain-1 space, increase in next double crochet) twice, double crochet in next double crochet, work Front Post double triple crochet as before, double crochet in next double crochet, increase in remaining double crochet; finish off.

Row 4: Join orange as before; work beginning increase, **[**double crochet in next 5 stitches (**working in top of Front Post double triple crochet same as in each double crochet**), increase in next double crochet, chain 1, skip next chain-1 space, increase in next double crochet**]** twice, double crochet in next 5 stitches, increase in remaining double crochet; finish off.

Row 5: Join medium yellow same as orange; work beginning increase, (double crochet in next double crochet, work Front Post double triple crochet around post of second double crochet of increase 2 rows **below**, double crochet in next 3 double crochets, work Front Post double triple crochet around post of first double crochet of next increase 2 rows **below**, double crochet in next double crochet, increase in next double crochet, chain 1, skip next chain-1 space, increase in next double crochet) twice, double crochet in next double crochet, work Front Post double triple crochet, double crochet in next 3 double crochets, work Front Post double triple crochet, double crochet in next double crochet, increase in remaining double crochet; finish off.

Row 6: Join medium yellow as before; work beginning increase, (double crochet in next 9 stitches, increase in next double crochet, chain 1, skip next chain-1 space, increase in next double crochet) twice, double crochet in next 9 stitches, increase in remaining double crochet; finish off.

Weave in yarn ends.

Finishing

With 2 motifs **wrong** sides together, thread tapestry or yarn needle with medium yellow and join in first double crochet to left of any chain-1 space. Sew edges together carefully matching stitches to next chain-1 space; finish off.

Join 42 motifs to form 6 strips of 7 motifs each.

Join 30 motifs to form 5 strips of 6 motifs with 1 half motif at each end.

Join strips in same manner as motifs, working thru all 3 chain-1 spaces where 3 motifs meet.

Piece should look like ***Figure 4***.

Figure 4

Edging

With piece **right** side facing, join medium yellow with slip stitch in first double crochet to left of chain-1 space marked A in ***Figure 4***.

Round 1: Working around entire afghan, beginning with top edge, work beginning increase, double crochet in next 11 double crochets, increase in next double crochet, chain 1, **†** ★ increase in next double crochet, double crochet in next 12 double crochets, **decrease in inside corner as follows**: yarn over, (pull up a loop in next chain-1 space) twice, (yarn over and draw thru 2 loops) 3 times **(decrease made)**, double crochet in next 12 double crochets, increase in next double crochet, chain 1; repeat from ★ 5 times **more**, increase in next double crochet, double crochet in next 11 double crochets, increase in next double crochet, chain 1, increase in next double crochet, double crochet in next 12 double crochets, chain 1, double crochet in next double crochet, (2 double crochets around post of last double crochet at end of next row on Half Motif) 5 times, double crochet in center space of Half Motif, (2 double crochets around post of last double crochet at end of next row on Half Motif) 5 times, double crochet in next double crochet, chain 1, double crochet in next 13 double crochets on next Motif, chain 1, continue to work each Motif and each Half Motif in same manner to last Motif on long side of afghan, double crochet in next 12 double crochets on side of last Motif, increase in next double crochet, chain 1 **†**, increase in next double crochet, double crochet in next 11 double crochets, increase in next double crochet, chain 1; repeat from **†** to **†** once; join with slip stitch in third chain of beginning chain-3; finish off.

Tassel Instructions (Make 14)

Cut a piece of cardboard 10" long and 6" wide. For each tassel, wind yarn loosely 30 times around 10" length. Cut a piece of yarn 20" long, double it and thread into yarn needle. Thread under all strands at top of cardboard and pull up tightly; knot securely. Cut at opposite side of cardboard ***(Figure 5)***. Cut another strand of yarn 10" long and wrap tightly twice around tassel 1½" below top knot. Knot; let excess fall in as part of tassel. Tie 1 tassel in chain-1 space at center of each point on top and bottom edges of afghan.

Figure 5

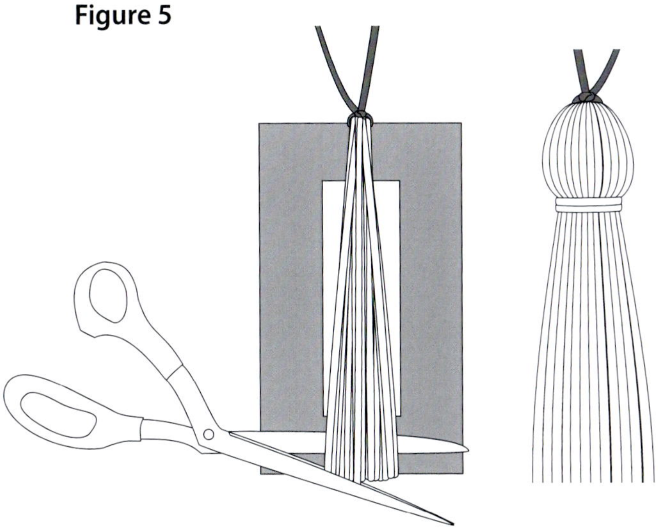

VERSION B *(Shown on page 8)*

MATERIALS

Worsted weight yarn, 16 ounces (454.4 grams) ecru, 42 ounces (1192.8 grams) assorted colors; aluminum crochet hook size H (Canadian size 5) **or** size needed for gauge.

GAUGE: In double crochet, 4 stitches = 1"; 2 rows = 1"
Rounds 1-6 = 6¼" x 8" hexagon

INSTRUCTIONS

Hexagon Motif (Make 72)

Round 1: With desired center color, follow instructions for VERSION A Hexagon Motif Round 1, page 9; at end of round, finish off.

Round 2: Join second color in first double crochet to left of any chain-1 space, work same as VERSION A Round 2.

Rounds 3-6: Joining new color each round and using ecru for Round 6, work same as VERSION A Rounds 3-6.

Half Motif (Make 10)

Using a different color for each row and ecru for Row 6, work same as VERSION A Half Motif.

Finishing

Following VERSION A Finishing instructions, join motifs and work edging with ecru.

Following Basic Fringe Instructions on page 12, cut 14" strands of ecru.
Using 3 strands for each knot, tie 1 knot in each chain-1 space and in every other double crochet across each short end.

Alternate Color Schemes

Alternate #1

Yarn Requirements: Worsted weight yarn, 32 ounces (908.8 grams) medium blue and 28 ounces (795.2 grams) white.

Working Instructions: Work Rounds 1-4 in white, Rounds 5 and 6 in medium blue. Joining, edging and fringe in medium blue.

Alternate #2

Yarn Requirements: Worsted weight yarn, 36 ounces (1022.4 grams) coral and 22 ounces (624.8 grams) rust.

Working Instructions: Work Rounds 1, 2, 4 and 6 in coral, Rounds 3 and 5 in rust. Joining and edging in coral. Tassels in rust.

GENERAL INSTRUCTIONS

GAUGE

Correct gauge is essential for proper size of items. Hook sizes given in instructions are merely guides and should never be used without first making a swatch to check gauge. To test gauge, make a sample swatch approximately 4" square in the stitch, yarn and hook specified. Then measure it, counting your stitches and rows carefully. If you have more stitches per inch than specified, try again with a larger size hook; if fewer, try again with a smaller size. Keep trying until you find the size that will give you the specified gauge.

DO NOT HESITATE TO CHANGE HOOK SIZE TO OBTAIN CORRECT GAUGE.

Conversion Chart
1 ounce = 28.4 grams
$1^{1}/_{2}$ ounce = 42.6 grams
2 ounce = 56.8 grams
$3^{1}/_{2}$ ounce = 28.4 grams
4 ounce = 113.6 grams

BASIC FRINGE INSTRUCTIONS

Cut a piece of cardboard about 8" wide and half as long as specified in instructions for finished strands. Wind yarn loosely around cardboard, cut across one end when card is filled. Repeat several times and then start fringing; you can wind more strands as you need them.

Fringe with **wrong** side of work facing you. Hold the number of strands specified for 1 knot of fringe together and fold in half. With crochet hook ***(Figure 7)*** draw folded end thru space or stitch, pull loose ends thru folded sections and draw knot up tightly ***(Figure 8)***.

Repeat, spaced as specified in individual instructions. Trim ends evenly.

Figure 6

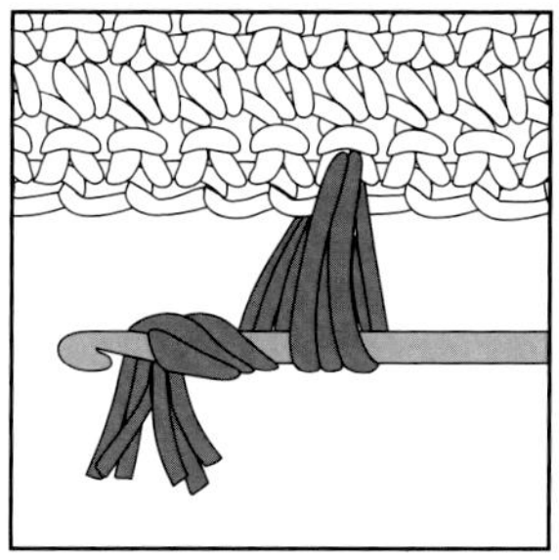

Figure 7

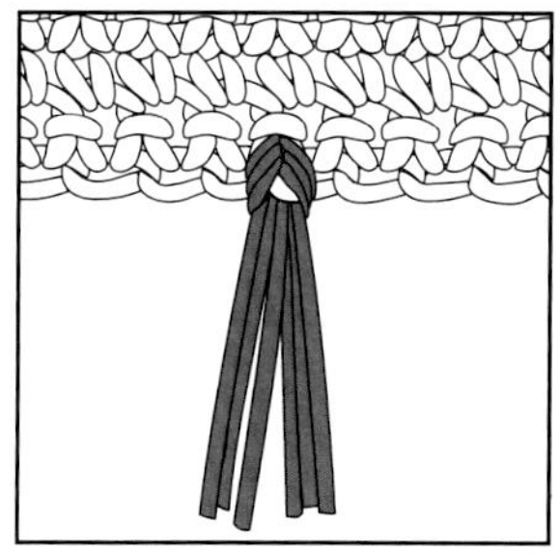

Made in U.S.A.